Enter His Gates

ps.100:4

To Your Jewish Roots

Susan Marcus

Art & Design: Studio Berenstine

Printed in Israel

T-land Ltd.
Tel.+972-4-671 2073
Fax. +972-4-671 2128
Toll Free to Israel: 1-866-820-2628
E-mail: mail@jesusboat.com
www.Jesusboat.com

Table of Contents

Introduction

Psalm 100. A Psalm of thanksgiving.
Make a joyful noise unto the Lord, all the earth. Serve the Lord with gladness: come before His presence with singing. Know that the Lord He is God: it is He who made us, and we belong to Him; we are His people, and the sheep of His pasture. Enter into His gates with thanksgiving and into His courts with praise: be thankful to Him and bless His name. For the Lord is good; His steadfast love endures forever; and His faithfulness to all generations.

In Psalm 100 we are reminded of the unique relationship between Man and God. To celebrate the relationship, we sing, we worship, we recognize His reign over all creation.

This is a book that has come into being to recognize how, why, and with what we can celebrate our relationship with the Almighty. It is not a treatise on Judaism. It is not the penultimate explanation of all things Jewish. It is simply a guide...a guide to the Jewish roots, the crucible, from which Jesus emerged. The celebrations today, including various items used at the celebrations are just the same today as they were in Jesus' day.

Contained within these pages are tools for you to use to "enter His gates". The explanations of various items traditionally found in Jewish homes are for you to use and enjoy. Recently, many Christians from various denominations have expressed interest in understanding these items. Therefore this book came into being. You, too, as a Christian, are invited to incorporate these items into your homes. Since all of these items existed also in Jesus' day and were part of his daily and holiday celebration, they can only help you deepen your spiritual walk.

Now to be truthful, maybe matza balls weren't around then but I thought that it would be fun to include in this guide some recipes, some games, some light thoughts as well. Enjoy!

We are indeed a privileged generation. Things about which our parents and grandparents could only read, pray, or dream, we get to do! First and foremost, we get to fulfill the Biblical injunction that says: "Get you up unto the land, and walk the length and breadth of it". Today, in the 21st century, every pilgrim can come to the Holy Land, to explore, to wander, and to pray at the very sites wherein the Bible unfolded.

So, also, are we today able to study the life and times of Jesus on location. From the shores of the Sea of Galilee to the heady atmosphere of the Holy City of Jerusalem, the Christian pilgrims today can share the same experiences. Echoes of history rise as a lacy cloud above the still waters of the Sea of Galilee. Faint words of prayer hang in the air around the ancient olive trees of the Garden of Gathsemene. Time is frozen. Ancient footfalls follow our every step throughout the Land.

Every step, every road sign, every olive tree reminds us of the days of the Bible. May your walk be enriched. May you go from strength to strength.

In the words of Proverbs 3:6 In all thy ways, acknowledge Him and He shall direct thy paths.

Acknowledgements

Dr. Ben Alpert of Boynton Beach, Florida has been actively involved in both the Jewish and Christian communities of the United States his entire adult life. Tirelessly traveling from congregation to congregation teaching, explaining, and inspiring, Ben has brought the message of the Bible to thousands. It was his concept to bring together all the questions raised over and over again at his presentations. It has been his dream to show the Christian world the beauty of early Biblical practice and to show that "You don't have to be Jewish!" to enjoy these items. Rather, you can incorporate them into your worship on a daily or weekly basis. I am deeply indebted to Ben for his encouragement, persistence, and confidence that I could bring forth something useful.

Alex Barak and Ohad Harpaz are two young Israelis of boundless energies, unlimited imagination, and dedication. They, their wives Tova and Na'ama, and their young families are the epitome of the success of the Jewish people. As sons of survivors of the Holocaust, they carry a special burden for the Jewish people. They are the living proof that God's word is eternal.... The Jewish people are an eternal people. Living in the Galilee, they have a store on the shores of the Sea of Galilee supplying "everything Jewish". From shofars to Bibles, from Biblically inspired jewelry to cosmetics, from books to banners, Alex and Ohad charm every customer with their interest, attention and good humor. Their belief in this book was the mortar holding all the various facets of production together.

Dahlia Berenstine designed and drew the illustrations on the pages of the text. Dahlia was born in Tel Aviv, grew up on Kibbutz Maoz Haim, and educated at the Polytechnic College in Tel Aviv. Today she has a studio for graphics and design in Ra'anana. Dahlia's works have been displayed at the Israeli parliament, the Knesset, as well as the White House in Washington, D.C. Many of her works are prized by the notables both here in Israel and abroad.

Bracha Lavee, one of Israel's premier artists, listened patiently as we (Ben, Alex, Ohad and I) tried to explain our vision for the cover.
The antiquity of the Jewish people. The olive tree with its gnarled roots inviting Christians to be grafted in. The city of Jerusalem. We wanted the feeling of entering the gates. It was very clear to us with her first sketch that Bracha understood completely. Bracha so deftly with her signature use of gold, draws us in through the gate to God's word. Bracha's works have been exhibited widely throughout Israel, the US, and Europe. It was a great honor to have her participate with us in this venture.

Devorah Alfasi of South Africa was instrumental at the very beginning of this venture for which we are greatly in her debt. She researched many items, designed graphics, and helped in layout.

Susan Marcus

Torah

התורה

Torah

"For thousands of years we safeguarded the Book, and it has kept us safe".

So wrote Israel's first prime minister, David Ben Gurion.

Indeed, the Bible given by God on Mount Sinai to Moses codified for all time the terms of the covenant entrusted to the Jewish people. Its laws and commandments describe a special relationship wherein God reveals Himself as a living, eternal, and covenant keeping God. God clearly outlines the blessings of following his instructions and the punishments for ignoring the laws. (Deuteronomy 11:13-17)

If we look at the Ten Commandments rather like the American Bill of Rights, then the expansion of these commandments, the Torah, is the Constitution of the Jewish people. These laws are meant to separate and sanctify the people as written in Leviticus 19:2, "You shall be holy, for I the Lord your God am holy".

"See, I have imparted to you laws and ordinances... Observe them faithfully for that will be proof of your wisdom and understanding in the sight of other peoples, who on learning of these laws, will say, "Surely this is a great nation of wise and understanding people... For what great nation is there, that has laws and ordinances as perfect as all this teaching that I set before you this day? (Deuteronomy 4:5-8)

But so many laws! There are 613 commandments in the Torah covering every single aspect of daily life ....religious, civil, business, and criminal. God assures us in Deuteronomy 30:11-14
"For this commandment which I command thee this day, it is not hidden from thee, neither is it far off.........But the word is very near to thee, in thy mouth, and in thy heart, that thou may do it."

Paul quotes this passage in Romans 10:4-8

The great sage, Hillel, was once asked by a young man, "If your Torah is so wonderful, tell it to me while I am standing on one foot." In response, Hillel replied "Do not unto others as you would not want them to do unto you. This is Torah. All the rest is commentary. Now go and study."

In actuality the word Torah means teaching. Its broadest meaning is the study of all spiritual and religious teaching.

The first five books of the Bible, Genesis, Exodus, Leviticus, Numbers, and Deuteronomy are known as the Torah. In Hebrew, the word is Chumash from the word for five. These books begin with the creation story and end with the death of Moses. It represents the teaching and will of God transferred to mankind through divine inspiration.

For over 3500 years, each word of Torah has been painstakingly copied letter for letter. Not a word has changed in all this time. Each word given to Moses at Sinai appears today exactly as it did then. So sacred are thought to be each jot and tittle that Jesus refers to its holiness in Matthew 5:17-18.

The expanded study of Torah includes also the writings and prophets. Together these three sections are called the Tenach forming the Bible.
Prophets contains the 21 books of the prophets while the Writings are the final books of the Bible, including Ezra and Nehemiah, Psalms, Job, and the five scrolls.

Menorah

המנורה

Menorah

Perhaps more than any other symbol, the menorah has come to represent the Jewish people. Today the symbol of the modern state of Israel, it once graced the Tabernacle as the children of Israel traveled through Sinai. It stood as a great monument in both the First and Second Temples. The instructions to build the menorah are clearly delineated in the Book of Exodus.

"And thou shalt make a candlestick of pure gold of beaten work shall the candlestick be made: his shaft, and his branches, his bowls, his knops, and his flowers, shall be of the same. And six branches shall come out of the sides of it; three branches of the candlestick out of the one side, and three branches of the candlestick out of the other side:

Three bowls made like unto almonds, with a knop and a flower in one branch; and three bowls made like unto almonds in the other branch, with a knop and a flower: so in the six branches that come out of the candlestick. And in the candlestick shall be four bowls made like unto almonds, with their knops and their flowers. And there shall be a knop under two branches of the same.... Their knops and their branches shall be of the same: all of it shall be one beaten work of pure gold. And thou shalt make the seven lamps thereof: and they shall light the lamps thereof, that they may give light over against it" (Ex. 25:31-37)

When the Romans destroyed the Second Temple, the general Titus, had his forces carry away the menorah as a symbol of the destruction of the Jewish people, Jerusalem, and the Temple. He later had it carved on the arch in Rome as an everlasting tribute to his victory.

However, the people still are here and for over three thousand years the menorah has been carved in stone, painted, decorated mosaic floors. Today it appears in Israel's courts, and is embossed on official stationery.

Throughout the centuries of exile, the Jewish people carried with them a menorah as a symbol of their history as well as confirmation in the eternal belief in God's word and the eventual redemption of the people together with their return to the land of Israel.

The prophet Zechariah had a vision described in Chapter 4:2-6

"I saw a menorah of gold...with seven lamps on it, with seven moldings in the seven lamps. There were two olive trees beside the menorah, one on each side of it. Then I asked the angel, 'What do these things mean, my lord?' And the angel said to me,

'Do you not know?' And I said, 'No, my lord.' Then he said, 'This is the word of the Lord unto Zerubavel:
Not by might nor by power, but by My spirit, says the Lord.'"

Zechariah, returning with the people from Babylonia understood the meaning of these words to be that the people of Israel were to be the "Light unto the world" as this saying was revealed to Zechariah in the seven flames of the menorah.

Whenever we look upon the menorah, we are reminded of God as the light of the world. The menorah stretches between the earthbound man and the purity and perfection of God. His light transcends all and beckons us toward higher ideals and holiness.

Mezuzah

המזוזה

Mezuzah

The mezuzah is a special object placed on the doorpost of a Jewish home.

It is a biblical commandment to place a mezuzah on each doorway to remember God's commandments and to live accordingly.

Inside the mezuzah, written by a scribe on parchment, are two portions of the book of Deuteronomy. The first is Deut. 6:4-9. This portion is known as the "watchword" of the Jewish faith, the "Shema". It says: "Hear, O Israel, the Lord our God, the Lord is one." It is followed by instructions to speak these words in many situations each day. The second portion on the parchment is from Deuteronomy 11:13-21. The intervening portions are various commandments culminating in the illuminating words of God's promise to the Jewish people. He tells us that if we follow His ordinances, God will deliver the beneficent rains in their seasons, the former rains and the latter rains, and prosperity in the land given to His people.

There are no rules, however, how the case that holds the parchment should look. Therefore, some are ceramic, or glass, or wood, or silver according to your desire. Some are modern, some classic. The variety is unlimited.

One consistent feature of every mezuzah, however simple or ornate is the Hebrew letter "Shin". Shin is the abbreviation of God's most mystical name, Shaddai. Sometimes the complete word of Shin, Daled, Yod is spelled out, and it stand for "Shomer D'latot Yisrael", the guardian of the gates of israel.

It is proper to put a mezuzah on the right hand side of each doorway both outdoors and inside, with the exception of bathrooms.

It is traditional that a person will touch a mezuzah when entering or exiting a building. It reminds us of the "Shema" and the commandment "to love God with all your heart, with all your soul, and all your might".

Your mezuzah does not need to be "kosher". That is to say, the symbolism of the mezuzah is fulfilled even if you place a printed scripture portion on paper inside the case. You need not go to the expense of a scribe written parchment.

Should you want to make a ceremony of affixing the mezuzah to your doorpost, the blessing is as follows:

ברוך אתה ה׳ אלוהינו מלך העולם אשר קדשנו
במצוותיו וצוונו על קביעת מזוזה.

Baruch Ata Adonai Eloheinu Melech Haolam asher kidshanu b'mizvotav v'zivanu al kviat mezuzah.

Blessed are You, O Lord our God, King of the Universe, who has sanctified us with His commandments and commanded us to affix a mezuzah.

Having a mezuzah on your door, touching it and then touching your lips, will remind you to keep the word of God on your lips as you enter and leave your home.

Kippah

כיפה

Skullcap

The wearing of a skullcap, known in Hebrew as "kippah" (kee-pah') or in Yiddush as "yarmulka" is not a biblical commandment.

There are no specific rules as to size, color, or fabric. Some are plain, some are decorated. The "knitted Kippah" is usually crocheted, sometimes with designs. It is a popular tradition among the observant community of Jews that a young woman will crochet a special kippah for her fiancé. One clue: the more plain, or black, is usually an indication of stricter religious observance though not always.

Today, the kippah worn by young boys and men at all times is an outward sign of a religiously observant Jew. It reminds him that he is earthbound and there is a far greater authority above him. It tells the world that he is bound by God's commandments and lives his life accordingly.

Sources show evidence of the wearing of a headcovering by Jewish males as early as the second century.

When entering a synagogue, all men and boys wear a kippah for the prayer service in reverence for the House of God. It is also worn at weddings, funerals, etc.

There is no reason a non-Jewish man cannot wear a kippah.

"Pray and seek my face..."

"when they sought Him,
     he was found..."

2 Chr. 7:14
15:4

Tallit

טלית

Prayer Shawl

The tallit, or prayer shawl, is the most recognizable sign of Jewish worship. It is worn by men from the age of BarMitzvah. Actual law proscribes from marriage but the tradition has evolved from the age of thirteen.

The tallit is usually made from either silk or wool. For many observant Jews, the use of wool is most important. Seeing the Almighty as the shepherd taking care of sheep whom He loves, the man wrapping himself in the shawl is actually wrapping himself also in the love of God as he prays.

The stripes on the tallit are usually blue or black. The blue is reminiscent of the special blue used in the fringes of the tallit in Biblical days, techelet, which came from a very rare snail found occasionally along the Mediterranean coastline near the modern city of Tel Aviv in Israel. Some tradition says that when using the black stripes on the tallit, it reminds us of the destruction of the Temple and the dispersion among the nations following the exile.

Today, the flag of Israel is sometimes seen in the design of the tallit with the two stripes of blue and a Star of David in the middle. In fact, the first flag of Israel was indeed a tallit onto which the Star of David was sewn!

The religious significance of the Tallit lies particularly in the Tzitzit , or fringes, at each of its four corners. Numbers 15:37-41 is the specific instruction for placing fringes on the corners.

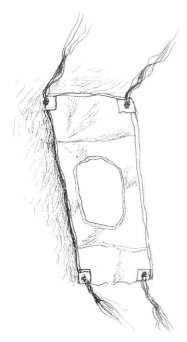

And the Lord spoke unto Moses saying: "Speak unto the children of Israel, and bid them that they make throughout their generations a fringe upon the corners of their garments, and that they put with the fringe of each corner a thread of blue. And it shall be unto you for a fringe, that you may look on it, and remember all the commandments of the Lord, and do them; and that you go not about after your own heart and your own eyes, after which you go astray."

Along the upper rim of the Tallit a ribbon is sewn on which is written the blessing recited when donning the Tallit.

ברוך אתה ה׳ אלוהינו מלך העולם אשר קדשנו במצוותיו וצוונו להתעטף בציצית.

Baruch Ata Adonei Eloheinu Melech Haolam asher kidshanu bmitzvotav vtzivanu ltatef bzizit.

Blessed are You, O Lord our God, King of the universe who has sanctified us with His commandments and commanded us to wrap ourselves in the tzitzit.

When is it worn?

The Tallit is worn only at prayer, or a groom at his wedding. It is worn at all morning services during the week as well as on Shabbat and holidays. It is also worn at the opening evening service of the holiday of Yom Kippur. Only on Yom Kippur is the tallit worn in the evening.

The design and color of the Tallit today is purely of personal choice. Some have geometric designs, some the skyline of Jerusalem, some are beautifully handwoven, whatever your taste.

There would be no requirement for you, as a Christian, to wear the Tallit. You may want to own one and wear it during your own personal time of prayer remembering the many psalms that refer to the Tallit as the shelter of the wings of God. You may want to purchase one for the classroom to teach on the prayer shawl or the teaching of the book of Numbers.

Shofar

שׁוֹפָר

Shofar

The shofar, or ram's horn, is a unique form of instrument. Although individual notes on a scale cannot be played on it, the combination use of long and short blasts can form a melody of sorts.

It can be long and curled or short with just a hint of a curve. The natural and polished finishes give a beautiful patina to each shofar. You will never find two exactly alike.

In Biblical days, the shofar was used in a variety of ways: The first and most important was to announce the onset of the beginning of the Sabbath and holidays. This was in pre-calendar days when people couldn't always be sure when the festival would begin.

It would be used at the coronation of a king, or as a sound to rally to battle.

It was used by Gideon (Judges 6 & 7) to confound the enemy, the Midianites, who so outnumbered Gideon's 300 men. It was used by Joshua to bring down the walls of Jericho!

The first reference we have of the use of the shofar in Scripture is when God called Moses to the summit of Mt. Sinai.

Today, the most important time of the year to use the shofar is at the New Year, Rosh HaShanah. In fact, one name for Rosh HaShanah is the Day of the Blowing of the Shofar. On this day it is blown 100 times in proscribed order.

There are three basic "notes" to the shofar. "Tekiah" is a long, drawn-out sound. "Shevarim" is a broken series of sounds. Finally, "T'ruah" is a series of sharp, staccato bursts.

On the holiest day of the year, Yom Kippur, the Day of Repentance, the shofar is blown only once, at the end of the 25 hour fast.

It makes a lot of sense for you to own a shofar since it also played an integral part in Jesus' life and is mentioned by name at least three times in the New Testament.

Matthew 24:31 — And He will send forth His angels with a great shofar and they will gather together His elect from the four winds, from one end of the sky to the other.

1 Corinthians 15:52 — In a moment, in the twinkling of an eye, at the last shofar; for the shofar will sound, and the dead will be raised imperishable, and we shall be changed.

1 Thessalonians 4:16 — For the Lord Himself will descend from heaven with a shout, with the voice of the archangel, and with the shofar of God.

Enjoy this wonderful instrument which evokes so many biblical themes, not the least of which is the ram caught in the thicket which Abraham used as a sacrifice in place of his son, Isaac.

More and more, we find churches incorporating the use of the shofar at the beginning of Sunday services, calling the congregation to prayer. How fitting to use the same instrument with which Jesus was also called to prayer.

Shabbat

שבת

Shabbat

שבת שלום

Shabbat

Remember the Sabbath day, to keep it holy.

Six days shalt thou labour, and do all thy work;

But the seventh day is a Sabbath unto the Lord thy God, in it thou shalt not do any manner of work, thou, nor thy son, nor thy daughter, nor thy man-servant, nor thy maid-servant, nor thy cattle, nor thy stranger that is within thy gates;

For in six days the Lord made heaven and earth, the sea and all that is in them, and rested on the seventh day; wherefore the Lord blessed the Sabbath day, and hallowed it.

Exodus 20:8 - 11

It has been said that "More than the Jews have kept the Sabbath, the Sabbath has kept the Jews".

This is a unique gift to the nation of Israel by God . It is so important that it is remembered as the fourth of the Ten Commandments.

"Remember the Sabbath day and keep it holy."

The Sabbath is the highlight of the week, often called the Sabbath Queen. Special foods are prepared. Best china and linen are used. The family gathers together for a special time of rest and sharing.
So often in the modern world people think that keeping the Sabbath is a list of "Don'ts". Don't write. Don't work. Don't iron. Don't travel. Don't use the telephone or electricity.
When truly experiencing the Sabbath, you will find it a great revelation that it is a day of refreshing "Do's".
Do spend time with the family. Do relax and read. Do study the portion of the week of the Torah. Do enjoy the slower pace and relaxation. Do join the community in celebration of the Sabbath in the synagogue. Do enjoy the special foods and atmosphere.

From the entry of the Sabbath at sundown of Friday afternoon to the ending of the Sabbath one hour after sundown (or when three stars can be seen in the sky), the atmosphere is permeated with joy, good will, rest, and, most importantly, spiritual renewal.

A Day of Love
The Sabbath is the great day of love — the shared hours
wherein fathers, mothers, and children learn to walk together,
holding hands, uplifting minds, teaching their tongues the
gladness their hearts must know.
Stuart E. Rosenberg

Sabbath Candles

Traditionally, the mother of the home lights the Sabbath candles. They are usually two silver candlesticks although they could be crystal, ceramic, or any other material.

The candles themselves are long burning and last between five and six hours, giving a radiant glow to the home all evening.

The mother then lights the right hand candle with a match and uses that candle to light the second one.

She covers her eyes as she recites the following blessing:

ברוך אתה ה׳ אלוהינו מלך העולם אשר קדשנו במצוותיו וצוונו להדליק נר של שבת.

Baruch ata adonai, eloheinu melech ha'olam, asher kidshanu b'mitzvotav, v'tzivanu l'hadlik ner shel Shabbat.

Blessed are you, O Lord our God, King of the Universe, who has sanctified us through His commandments and commanded us to kindle the Sabbath candles.

Blessing the Children
Families gather around the Sabbath table and the father and mother bless their children by placing a hand on the head of each child and reciting. For daughters:

ישמח אלוהים כשרה רבקה רחל ולאה.

Yismech elohim k'sara,rivkah,Rachel,v'leah

May God make you as Sarah, Rebecca,Rachel, and Leah
For sons:

ישמח אלוהים כאפריים ומנשה.

Yis'mcha elohim k'efraim v'menashe

May God make you as Efraim and Menashe
Followed by:

יברכך ה' וישמרך. יאר ה' פניו אליך ויחנך, ישא ה' פניו אליך וישם לך שלום.
Y'varech'cha adonai v'yish'marecha. Yaer adonai panav elecha veechunecha. Yisah adonai panav elecha vyasim lecha shalom.

May the Lord bless you and guard over you. May the Lord shine His countenance upon you and be gracious unto you. May the Lord favor you and grant you peace.

Kiddush - Blessing over the wine

The blessing over the wine is recited by the head of the household. In his absence, the mother or any other adult can recite the blessing.

The wine goblet is filled with sweet, red wine..usually Concord grape in the US. After the blessing, the father takes a sip and everyone around the table also takes a sip.

ברוך אתה ה' אלוהינו מלך העולם בורא פרי הגפן.

Baruch ata adonai, eloheinu melech ha'olam boray pree hagefen.

Blessed are you, O Lord our God, King of the Universe, who creates the fruit of the vine.

What has been included here is the short blessing and perfectly acceptable. If you are interested in the full Sabbath benediction, it reads as follows:

It was evening and it was morning.

On the sixth day the heavens and the earth and all their hosts were completed. For by the seventh day God had completed his work which he had made, and he rested on the seventh day from all his work which he had made. Then God blessed the seventh day and hallowed it, because on it he rested from all his work which God had created to function thenceforth. Genesis 2:2-3

Blessed are you, O Lord our God, King of the universe, who has sanctified us with His commandments and has been pleased with us; in love and favor has given us His holy Sabbath as a heritage, a memorial of the creation — that day being also the first among the holy festivals, in remembrance of the exodus from Egypt. You have chosen us and hallowed us above all nations, and in love and favor hast given us thy holy Sabbath as a heritage. Blessed are you, o Lord, who sanctifies the Sabbath.

Motzi

The blessing over the Challah , a special braided egg-rich bread is then recited. (See section on blessings…blessing over bread.)

"It shall be a sign for all time between Me and the people of Israel; for in six days the Lord made heaven and earth, and on the seventh day He ceased from work and rested." Exodus 31:17

Since this very special day was between God and Israel, it is the most important day to the Jewish people. Desecration of the Sabbath is considered a major transgression of God's word. Christians today are also discovering the joys of the seventh day as a day of rest. If you would like to incorporate the sanctity of the Sabbath traditions

as Jesus observed his entire life, you are most welcome.

The meals, the rest and the family time can only enhance your own traditions!!

The greeting to everyone on the Sabbath is :

Shabbat Shalom! A peaceful Sabbath.

The Sabbath Meal

Traditionally, the Sabbath meal is a very festive occasion. A typical menu for an Ashkenazi (European background) family would include:
Wine, Challah (the special egg-rich braided bread)
Chopped liver, chopped herring
Soup (chicken soup with noodles is the most popular)
Roast stuffed chicken with many vegetable side dishes
Dessert - a variety of cakes, cookies, fruit compote, etc.

Challah- makes three loaves

Mix together: 3 eggs, 1/2 c.(125ml) sugar, 6 Tbs. Vegetable oil, 1 Tbs. Salt, 1 1/2 c. (325ml)warm water, 2 pkgs. Fleischmann's yeast (regular or fast-rise). Add 6-8 c.(1 Kilo) flour (more if necessary to make soft, pliable dough. Can be made with mixmaster, switching to dough hook after first amounts of flour. Place dough in greased bowl. Cover and let rise in warm place away from drafts until double. (one to two hours) Punch down dough and let rise again — about one hour until double.

Place dough on work surface. Cut into three sections.

Divide each of the three sections also into three long rolls. Braid. Place in greased loaf pan 9x5(23cm x 13cm). Repeat with other two sections. Cover and let rise about 30-40 minutes.

Just before baking, brush tops of loaves with beaten egg.

Bake in 350 degree oven for 23 minutes until golden brown. Immediately turn out onto cooling rack.

Station guards around loaves so they won't disappear before dinner!!

Havdalah

הבדלה

Havdalah

Just as the Sabbath Queen is ushered in with grace and ceremony, so, too, do we bid goodbye to the Sabbath in a short service called Havdalah. Havdalah, in Hebrew, means to separate or divide. This service separates the Sabbath from the rest of the ordinary weekdays.

As we return to our daily routines, we hesitate to let go of the tranquility of the Sabbath. Therefore, many times, this service is a special time for families to be together to hold the service in the home with full participation of all in the household.

After nightfall, traditionally when three stars can be seen in the sky, the service commences using a wine goblet (kiddush cup), braided candle, and spice box filled with fragrant spices.

The family will gather together for Havdalah to separate the sacred spirit of the Sabbath from the secular week ahead. The spice box, candle, kiddush cup are divided among the family to hold.

The cup of wine is filled, the Havdalah candle is lit. The head of the family raises *the cup of wine (or grape juice) and recites:*

ברוך אתה ה׳ אלוהינו מלך העולם בורא פרי הגפן (שהכול נהיה בדברו)

Baruch ata adonai elohainu melech ha-olam borai pri hagafen (she-hakol Y'he-yeh bidvaro).

Blessed are you, O Lord our God, King of the universe who creates the fruit of the vine (by whose will all things exist).

The Spice Box with its rich, sweet fragrance is considered by sages to be uplifting for the soul, rather than the body to replace the filling of a spiritual "downer" as the Sabbath leaves.

The box is generally a very decorative object of silver, brass, wood, or even ceramic, artistically designed. It is called a "b'samim box". B'samim in Hebrew means spices. The box is raised the following blessing offered.

ברוך אתה ה׳ אלוהינו מלך העולם בורא מיני בשמים.

Baruch ata adonai elohainu melech has-olam borai minai b'samim.

Blessed are you, O Lord our God, King of the universe who creates diverse spices.

At the conclusion of this blessing, the spice box is passed around for all to smell.

Now it's time to use the Havdalah candle. Unlike the beautiful white Sabbath candles in traditional form, the Havdalah candle is not a regular candle. It is made of two or more braided wicks to form a large flame. It can be many sizes and colors. Usually, the youngest in the family likes to hold the candle during the service. All attention is focused on the candle and the following blessing is recited:

ברוך אתה ה׳ אלוהינו מלך העולם בורא מאורי האש.

Baruch ata adonai elohainu melech ha-olam borai m'orai ha-esh.

Blessed are you, O Lord our God, King of the universe who creates the lights of the fire.

The cup of wine is raised once again and the main blessing is recited:

ברוך אתה הי אלוהינו מלך העולם המבדיל בין קדש לחול, בין אור לחשך, בין ישראל לעמים, בין יום השביעי לששת ימי המעשה. ברוך אתה ה׳ המבדיל בין קדש לחול.

Baruch ata adonai, elohainu melech ha'olam, hamavdil bayn kodesh l'hol, bayn or l'hoshech, bayn Yisrael l'amim, bayn yom hashvi'I leshaishet y'may hamaaseh. Baruch ata adonai, hamavdil bayn kodesh l'hol.

Blessed are you, O Lord our God, King of the universe who makes a division between the sacred and secular, between light and darkness, between Israel and the other nations, between the seventh day and the six working days. Blessed art Thou, Lord, who makes a distinction between the sacred and the secular.

Customarily, the family then sings a song urging the prophet Elijah the Tishbite to come quickly in our day with the Messiah, son of David.

The
Twelve
Tribes

Asher

Naphtali

Menasseh

Zebulun

Issachar

Gad

Menasseh

Ephraim

Reuben

Binyamin

Dan

Shimon

Judah

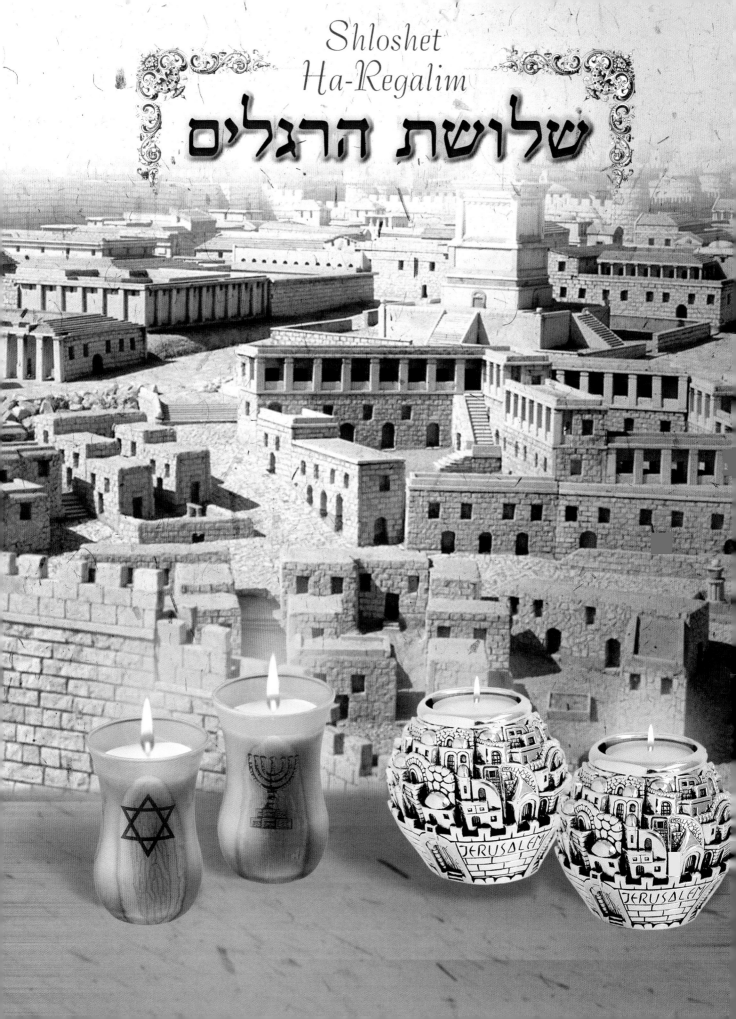

The Three Pilgrimage Festivals

Passover, "the time of our freedom" commemorates the Exodus from 400 years of slavery in Egypt.

Shavuot, "the time of the giving of our Torah" commemorates the revealing of the Torah on Mount Sinai and first fruits.

Sukkot , "the time of joy", is the Festival of Tabernacles.

Each of these festivals required the Jewish people to make a physical pilgrimage up to Jerusalem and the Temple.

It is said, "Each celebrant should come to Jerusalem three times a year, on these days. If one cannot come three times a year, one should come up to Jerusalem once a year. And, IF, one cannot come up to Jerusalem once a year, one should come up to Jerusalem once in a lifetime."

Indeed, in the days of Jesus, worshippers came up to the Holy City from the far corners of the world to celebrate. It would swell the city population to twice and perhaps three times its normal size. Each of the Gospels writes of Jesus coming up to fulfill this injunction at the time of Passover. The Book of Acts reports of the disciples in Jerusalem not only at Passover but also at the time of Shavuot (Pentecost). It was an important part of life to make the trek from Galilee up to Jerusalem to partake in the celebrations.

Even today, as the world becomes smaller with modern travel, the three pilgrimage festivals are the times when the most tourists come to the modern city of Jerusalem. At these times a cacophony of sounds and languages can be heard throughout the land.

Most particularly since 1980, the number of Christians from around the world coming to the Sukkot festival has grown each year to celebrate together with the people of Israel.

Pesach
פסח

Time of our Freedom
Passover

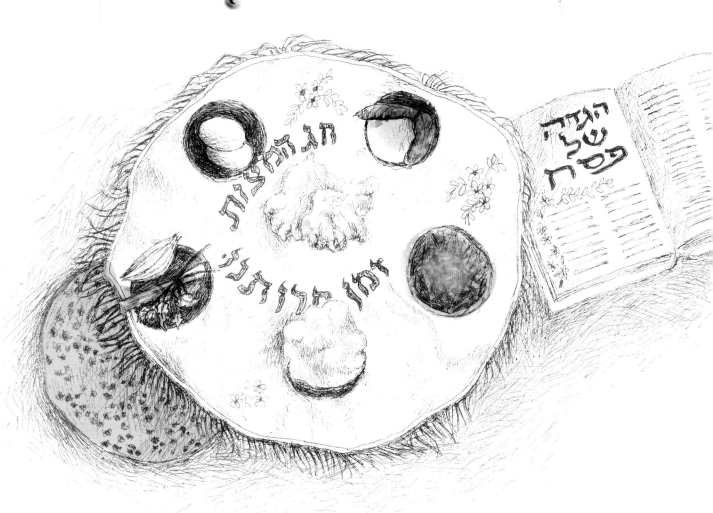

Every Passover, the Jewish people remember the miraculous events of God taking them out from slavery in Egypt unto freedom. It was in Sinai that God revealed himself to Moses for forty days and gave to the children of Israel the Ten Commandments and the Torah.

"And the Lord spoke unto Moses and Aaron in the land of Egypt, saying, This month shall be unto you the beginning of months: it shall be the first month of the year to you...And they shall eat the flesh in that night, roast with fire, and unleavened bread; and with bitter herbs they shall eat it...And this day shall be unto you for a memorial: and ye shall keep it a feast by an ordinance for ever. Seven days shall ye eat unleavened bread.... And ye shall observe this thing for an ordinance to thee and to they sons for ever. And it shall come to pass, when ye come to the land which the Lord will give you, according as he hath promised, that ye shall keep this service. And it shall come to pass, when your children shall say unto you, What mean ye by this service? That ye shall say, It is the sacrifice of the Lord's Passover, who passed over the houses of the children of Israel in Egypt, when he smote the Egyptians, and delivered our houses" (Exodus 12:1-27)

To observe all that God has commanded each year at the Festival of Passover, a special meal is held called a Seder. Seder means order. There is a prescribed order to the meal with prayer, food and drink.

Each person is to tell the story of Passover as if he himself had been redeemed. We recall the suffering at the hands of the Egyptians. We recall that God heard our prayers and took us out, as it is said, "with a mighty hand and an outstretched arm". Every generation is commanded to tell this story forever.

The actual telling of the story, at the Seder, is from a book called the Hagaddah, meaning to tell. Many symbols are used at this meal in order to make the telling a vivid story, always remembering that it is God who brings about redemption and not man.

A central theme in the telling of the liberation from slavery is asking of the "Four Questions", or "Why is this night different from all other nights?"

One of the main features on the Seder Table is the Seder Plate. It is a large plate with sections divided for various objects relating to the exodus.

Shankbone - Zeroah- A lamb shankbone is roasted and placed on the plate. This reminds the people of the 10th plague visited upon the Egyptians, the killing of the firstborn. people that they would need divine protection from this plague. He ordered them to take a lamb, slaughter it and then sprinkle its blood on the lintel and doorposts of every household. At midnight, the Angel of Death passed through Egypt, striking all the firstborn, and Egypt became the lowliest of nations whereas she had been the greatest, "so that Egypt may know that I am God." The children of Israel remained safe for God had told them "when I see the blood I will pass over you.. (EX. 12:13

Roasted egg - Baytzah- The egg is a symbol of new life just as Passover is celebrated in the Spring of the year as new life emerges from the long winter months. Despite any hardship, life continues with God's eternal blessings. The egg is also associated with mourning and at the Seder is a reminder of the destruction of the Temple which is always remembered at any joyous celebration.

Bitter Herbs - Maror- Today usually horseradish is used to represent the bitterness of slavery.

Karpas - Celery or parsley (any green herb, not bitter) also reminds of the Spring. Dipping the Karpas into a small bowl of salt water helps us remember our tears during slavery.

Charoset - Apples, nuts and wine (or in the Middle East, dates, nuts, and wine) are mixed together into a sweet paste. It reminds us of the mortar that was used to make the bricks in Egypt.

Wine - According to tradition, everyone must have no less than 4 cups of wine at the seder. These represent the four promises God gave of deliverance.
1.	I will bring you out .....from under the slavery of the Egyptians.
2.	I will deliver you.....from their bondage.
3.	I will redeem you.....with an outstretched arm
4.	I will take you as My people.

Cup of Elijah - a special wine goblet is placed on the table awaiting the arrival of Elijah the prophet.

Three Matzot - The three matzot are placed in a special decorative holder called a "Matzatash". Made from silk or other fabric, the leader of the seder places a single matzah in each of the three divisions of the holder. These represent the two loaves of bread which we always use on Shabbat and Yom Tov plus an additional one for the "Bread of Affliction". Some

say the three matzot also represent the three classes of the Jewish people: Kohanim, Levites, and Israelites.

During the telling of the Hagaddah, the middle matzah is removed from its compartment, lifted up, and broken in two. The larger piece is placed in a napkin and hidden by the leader of the seder. This is called the "afikoman" representing the Passover lamb that was eaten at the meal. Children try to find the afikoman in order to redeem it at the end of the meal for a special prize.

"These are the feasts of the Lord, even holy convocations, which ye shall proclaim in their seasons. In the fourteenth day of the first month at evening is the Lord's Passover. And on the fifteenth day of the same month is the feast of unleavened bread unto the Lord: seven days ye must eat unleavened bread...(Lev. 23:4-7)

Matzah is called the "bread of affliction". Because the Hebrews had to leave with Moses in great haste, there was no time to allow the bread to rise. For the entire holiday, no food is consumed that contains any leavening whatsoever. Homes are meticulously cleaned (the original spring housecleaning!) to remove every last crumb or vestige of leaven. Often, leavening is likened unto sin. When one is filled with self pride, importance, it leads to arrogance and ultimately, sin. The Egyptians were filled with self pride in their wealth and power.

By removing leavening from ourselves for a full seven days, it gives us time to reflect upon our commitment to God and to seek out and remove sin from the innermost corners of our being.

All the pageantry, symbolism, and ritual of the Passover Seder remind us that we are free men and no longer slaves.

Enjoyment of all the items surrounding the Passover meal such as the seder plate, the cup of Elijah, the matzah holder are constant reminders of the powerful events in the days of Moses.

The New Testament relates the Last Supper that Jesus shared with his disciples to be the Passover Seder. It is at this opportunity that Jesus shares the "New Covenant" using the Matzah and the wine to represent his body and his blood.

Having a community seder at the time of Passover helps congregations come closer to the teachings of Jesus.

No Passover Seder is complete without matzah ball soup. Below is my favorite recipe for matzah balls.

Light as air matzah balls

3 eggs, separated
3/4 c.(175ml) matzah meal
1/2 tsp. Salt

Beat egg whites until stiff. Fold in yolks, which have been beaten with the salt. Carefully but completely fold in the matzah meal. Let stand five minutes. Wet your hands and form balls. Drop into boiling soup stock or salt water. Cover and cook 35 minutes.
This will make 12 large balls.

Passover Sponge Cake

1 c.(250ml) cake meal	12 eggs, separated
1/4 c.(60ml) potato starch	1 lemon rind
1 1/2 c.(375ml) sugar	4 oz.(125ml) orange juice

Sift together cake meal and potato starch. Add sugar to well beaten egg yolks. Add grated lemon rind and orange juice. Fold in sifted meal. Mix well. Fold in stiffly beaten egg whites. Bake in an ungreased tube pan (10 in.) at 325 degrees for 1 hour.
Remove from oven. Invert pan and let cool another hour before removing from pan.

First Fruits to the Temple-Feast of Weeks
Shavuot

"The first of the firstfruits of thy land thou shalt bring into the house of the Lord thy God"... Ex. 23:19

Shavuot is the Hebrew word for weeks. It concludes the daily counting of the "omer" barley offering at the Temple. The count goes on for seven weeks. Beginning on the Second day of Passover, it is the 50th day, the holiday is known by Christians as Pentecost.

"When the Day of Pentecost had fully come, they were all with one accord in one place." Acts 2:1

At the offering of the first fruits not every species was represented. Rather only those fruits for which Israel is praised. "Wheat, barley, grapes, figs, pomegranates, olives, and dates" were brought to the Temple (Deut. 8:8)

The holiday also commemorates the giving of the Ten Commandments on Mount Sinai to Moses from the Lord.

The Shavuot holiday traditions observed today combine and symbolize both the agricultural and the religious importance of the festival. Homes are decorated with flowers to remember the blossoms of the Land of Israel. In the synagogue the Book of Ruth is read to describe the grain harvest in ancient days. Cheese cakes, honey cakes and other dairy food are eaten to remember the Land of Israel as it was described as a "land flowing with milk and honey."

Honey and milk are also symbols of Torah and learning. The sages describe the study of the word as being sweet as honey. In fact, many families, before discussing Torah at home will place a drop of honey on each child's tongue (including babies) so the children will always associate the learning of the Torah as sweet.

Food for Shavuot

It has become traditional to serve dairy dishes to celebrate the holiday of Shavuot. Two of the most popular are cheese blintzes and a noodle casserole called "kugel".

Blintzes
Batter -
1 1/2 c.(375ml) water, 2 eggs, 1 c. flour

Beat eggs well. Add water. Add flour and mix well. Heat 8" frying pan. Grease pan with a little margarine. Pour just enough batter in the pan to cover bottom thinly. Turn out crepe as soon as batter dries, onto a dish towel. Makes about 12 blintzes

Filling - Cheese
1 lb.(400-450gr) Farmer cheese   2 eggs
1/2 c.(125ml) sugar   1 Tbs. cinammon
1/2 c.(125ml)crushed pineapple.

Filling - Potato
3 boiled potatoes, mashed   1/2(100gr) stick margarine
1 1/2 Tb. Instant onion soup   pinch of salt, pepper

For both fillings - mix all ingredients together. Spoon filling mixture onto fried side of crepe and fold over into thirds and tuck sides in. Fry . These freeze very well.

Feast of Tabernacles
Sukkot

"And the Lord spoke unto Moses, saying, Speak unto the children of Israel, saying, The fifteenth day of this seventh month shall be the Feast of Tabernacles for seven days unto the Lord......
"And ye shall take you on the first day the boughs of goodly trees, branches of palm trees, and the boughs of thick trees, and willows of the brook......
"Ye shall dwell in booths seven days; all that are Israelites born shall dwell in booths. That your generations may know that I made the children of Israel to dwell in booths, when I brought them out of the land of Egypt: I am the Lord your God." (Lev. 23:33-34)

Immediately following the conclusion of the Day of Atonement, Yom Kippur, sounds of hammers and nails echo through the cold night air of Jerusalem as people begin to build their "Sukkah" or booth for the celebration of the Feast of Tabernacles.

Following the Levitical commandment to dwell in booths, the Jewish people build temporary dwellings to remind them of the booths in which the people dwelt in Sinai enroute to the Land of Israel.

Also significant for the holiday is the celebration of the harvest of the orchards and fields.

The lulav and etrog (citron) recall the ceremonies at the First and Second Temples at the feast of Tabernacles.

On the last day of Sukkot , called Simhat Torah, (The joy of the Torah) processions of worshippers march around the synagogue carrying the scrolls of the Torah.

The beauty of the Sukkot holiday is that it combines elements of historical, agricultural, and religious aspects of worshipping God.

Dairy products are the preferred menu on this holiday. Below is one of my family's favorites!

Noodle Kugel

1 box broad noodles	8oz. (225gr) cottage cheese
3 eggs, beaten	1/2 lb. (225gr) cream cheese
1/4 lb. (120gr) Butter	1/2 lb. (225gr) American cheese, cut up
1 c. (250ml) milk	1 c. (250ml) sour cream

Pour eggs over cooked noodles; add milk, cottage cheese, cream cheese, American cheese, sour cream, sugar and dash of cinnamon. Mix together gently. Add 1/8 lb. Butter (cut up). Place in a 9 x 13 (33 x 23cm) pan and spread crushed corn flakes on top. Dot with remaining butter.
Bake at 350 degrees for 1 - 1 1/2 hours.
Serve warm or cold with sour cream on the side.

Chanukah

חנוכה

The Festival of lights
Chanukah

Celebrated in November-December, Chanukah is the most widely observed holiday in the Jewish calendar. Called the festival of lights, it commemorates the victory of the Jewish people, led by the Maccabees, over the Greek Seleucid ruler, Antiochus the fourth.

In the year 164 b.c.e. the Greek ruler forbade the practice of Judaism including performing of rituals such as circumcision, observing the Sabbath, owning a Bible. Such was his power and self-confidence, he thought that by edict he could force the people to abandon their belief in God. To that end, he also brought pigs and idols into the Temple in Jerusalem.

He misunderstood the nature of the Jewish people. Antiochus might have had a better chance of victory if he simply left the people alone and let the Greek culture inculcate itself into society. Since to be modern in those days was to be Greek, or a Hellenist, many Jews were succumbing to the temptation of the Greek way of life.

He thought he could impose Hellenism on the people, but he hadn't counted on one family living in a little town called Modi'in.
At the head of the family was a man called Mattathias. Together with his five sons, he rallied the people to rise up against the Greeks and preserve the Jewish people. With the slogan, "Mi L'adonai, acherai", ("Whoever is for the Lord, follow me"), a rebellion began against the most incredible odds. Mattathias and his sons, called Maccabees (meaning Hammer) defeated the Greeks and reconquered Jerusalem.

To their horror, they found the Temple in Jerusalem totally desecrated. They cleansed the Temple, removing the idols and swine but found in the eternal light only enough oil to last for one day. It would take 8 days to replenish the light. Miraculously, the little cruse of oil lasted for eight days until the new oil could be brought.

The total rebellion lasted for three years but, in the end, when the Maccabees were successful, they had fought the first war for religious freedom in the history of mankind. At the time of this battle, the Jews were the only monotheists in the world! Because the Temple was cleansed and God performed a miracle in allowing the oil to last for eight days, the rededication of the Temple gave the name Chanukah to the celebration.

Also known as the Feast of Lights, we light candles in a special candelabrum called a Chanukiah for eight nights.

The Chanukiah

To commemorate the Festival of Lights, we light a special candelabrum called a Chanukiah. It is different from a menorah. Unlike the seven branched menorah, the Chanukiah has nine branches.

There are eight candles on one level and a ninth candle, called the shammash either on the same level or perhaps standing higher. The ninth candle, the shammash lights the other candles. One additional candle is lit each night to remember God's miracle of the oil until on the last night all candles are burning brightly.

While the additional lights are added from right to left, the candles are lit from left to right.

There are no dictates as to the size, shape, design, material used to make the Chanukiah. They can be modern, traditional, silver, bronze, ceramic, renaissance, juvenile, etc. The only "law" to make the Chanukiah "kosher" is that eight of the candles be on equal level while the shammash can be of any height.

The candles are lit just after sundown and burn for at least 30 minutes.

The following blessings are then recited:

ברוך אתה ה׳ אלוהינו מלך העולם אשר קדשנו במצוותיו וצוונו להדליק נר של חנוכה.

Baruch ata adonai, eloheinu melech hao'lam, asher kidshanu b'mitzvotav, v'tzivanu l'hadlik ner shel Chanukah.

Blessed are you, O Lord our God, King of the Universe, who has commanded us to kindle the Chanukah light.

ברוך אתה ה׳ אלוהינו מלך העולם שעשה ניסים לאבותינו בימים ההם בזמן הזה.

Baruch ata adonai, eloheinu melech ha'olam she'asah nissim l'avoteinu, b'yamim hahem , b'zman hazeh

Blessed are you, O Lord our God, King of the Universe, who performed miracles for our forefathers in those days, at this time.

On the first night only, the shehechiyanu blessing (see chapter on blessings) is added.

ברוך אתה ה׳ אלוהינו מלך העולם שהחיינו וקיימנו והגיענו לזמן הזה.

Baruch ata adonai, eloheinu melech ha'olam, shehechiyanu, v'kiyamanu, v'higiyanu, l'zman hazeh.

Blessed are you, O Lord our God, King of the Universe who has kept us in life, and sustained us, and allowed us, to reach this moment.

Playing Dreidl

A dreidl is a small top with which children play during Chanukah. In Hebrew it is called a Sevivon.

The dreidl is four-sided with a Hebrew letter painted on each side.
The Hebrew letters, Nun, Gimmel, Heh, Peh are the first letters of the following sentence Nes Gadol Haya Poh, meaning a great miracle happened here. In America, and outside Israel, the fourth letter Peh, is replaced with a shin for the word Sham, meaning a great miracle happened there.

How to play.
Children (or adults!) sit around the table with the dreidl. Everyone is given a supply of toothpicks (kids much prefer jelly bean tokens!) Everyone places a jelly bean in the center of the table.
The first player spins. According to the letter appearing on top when the dreidl stops, the following occurs:

Nun. The player neither puts in nor takes out a jelly bean.
Gimmel. The player takes all the jelly beans. Players then place a jelly bean again in the center of the table and play continues.
Heh. The player takes half the jelly beans on the table.
Peh or Shin. The player puts in a jelly bean

The Food and Fun of Chanukah

To remember the miracle God performed with the tiny cruse of oil, the Jewish people celebrate the Festival by eating foods deep fried in oil such as doughnuts, potato pancakes (latkes) etc.

Potato Pancakes (Latkes)

10-12 potatoes, peeled and grated *
2 large onions, peeled and grated *
2 eggs
1 tbs. salt
1/2 to 1 c. (125-250ml) flour
2 tsp. baking powder
1 tsp. baking soda
pepper, garlic to taste.

*Hand grating is still the best method for grating the potatoes. If, however, you prefer to use the food processor, pulse the potatoes so they don't become too mushy.

After grating the potatoes, drain excess moisture. Add onions and rest of ingredients. Add the flour at the end ...just enough to hold mixture together.

Fry in deep, hot vegetable oil until crisp and golden brown on each side. Drain on paper towels. Serve with applesauce and/or sour cream.

Forget the calories. Chanukah comes but once a year!

The celebration of Chanukah is one feast you can enjoy from beginning to end...the menorah, the candles, the songs, the foods, the games. Since Chanukah came into being almost two centuries before Jesus, we can be assured that Jesus also celebrated the holiday. Indeed, the New Testament records Jesus celebrating Chanukah in Jerusalem! (John 10:22).

Since Chanukah falls in December, many people mistakenly think Chanukah is the "Jewish" Christmas. Nothing could be further from the truth! In fact, Chanukah commemorates the Jews' refusal to assimilate into a foreign culture!!

"Pray for the Peace of Jerusalem"
Ps 122/6

Purim

פורים

Purim

אֲרִי

לְהִי בִּימֵי אֲחַשְׁוֵרוֹשׁ הוּא אֲחַשְׁוֵרוֹשׁ הַמֹּלֵךְ

רְדּוֹ וְעַד כּוּשׁ שֶׁבַע וְעֶשְׂרִים וּמֵאָה מְדִינָה,

הֶם כְּשֶׁבֶת הַמֶּלֶךְ אֲחַשְׁוֵרוֹשׁ עַל כִּסֵּא

אֲשֶׁר בְּשׁוּשַׁן הַבִּירָה בִּשְׁנַת שָׁלוֹשׁ

עָשָׂה מִשְׁתֶּה לְכָל שָׂרָיו וַעֲבָדָיו חֵיל פָּרַס

פַרְתְּמִים וְשָׂרֵי הַמְּדִינוֹת לְפָנָיו בְּהַרְאֹתוֹ

שֶׁר כְּבוֹד מַלְכוּתוֹ וְאֶת יְקָר תִּפְאֶרֶת גְּדוּלָתוֹ

Purim

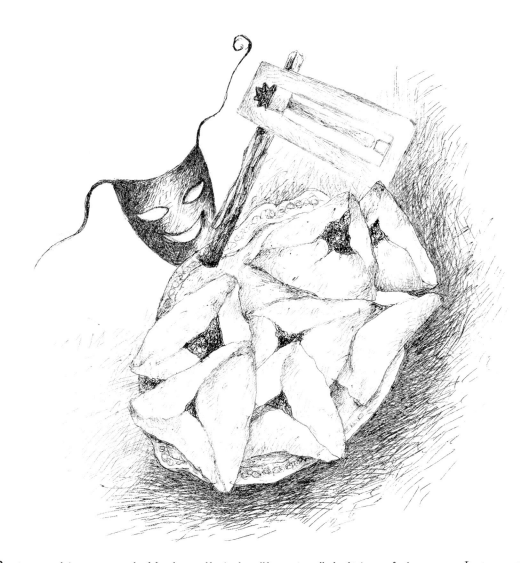

Purim could most probably be called the "happiest" holiday of the year. It is a time for donating gifts for the poor, for exchanging gifts with family and friends, for dressing up in costumes and, generally, rejoicing in the wonderful story contained in the Book of Esther.

Purim commemorates events in Persia and Medina. There, about two hundred years B.C.E., an evil man by the name of Haman had a plan to destroy the Jews. He drew lots to decide the date - the 14th of the Hebrew month Adar. The word "purim" in Hebrew means lots - therefore the name of the holiday.

For full details, read the Book of Esther! It's a story of mystery and intrigue as Queen Esther and her uncle, Mordecai, uncover and foil Haman's plot saving the entire Jewish population. Instead, on the day Haman and his conspirators planned to hang the Jewish people of Shushan, he and his henchmen were hanged!

In the synagogue on the evening of Purim and on the following morning, the entire Book of Esther is read. Everyone is provided with or brings their own noisemaker so that whenever Haman's name is mentioned, the congregants will drown out his name.

Children dress up in costumes, most often as characters of the Book of Esther.

Gifts of food and pastries are exchanged featuring Hamantaschen (ha-man-tash-en), or Haman's ears.

An interesting note: The Book of Esther is the only book of the Bible wherein God's name is not mentioned.

Enjoying the holiday:

The special food that is prepared on Purim is called Hamantaschen. It is a delightful triangular shaped pastry which in America is called, Haman's hat, and in Israel, called Haman's ears.
Two of my favorite recipes for these cakes are as follows:

Yeast Hamentaschen

2 pkg.(50gr) fresh yeast   1 c.(250ml) water
1/4c.(60ml) lukewarm water   5 c.(1250ml) sifted flour
1 tsp. salt   3 eggs, beaten
1/2(120gr) melted shortening   egg for glaze

Soften yeast in lukewarm water. Add salt, sugar, and shortening. Add 2 c. flour; beat well. Add yeast and eggs. Add remaining flour to make a soft dough. Knead on a lightly floured board until shiny.
(also works well with dough hook of mixer) Place in lightly greased bowl. Cover. Let rise until doubled. Punch down and gather into a ball. (At this point can be refrigerated overnight if desired).

Divide dough into medium-sized balls. Roll out to rounds 1/4 inch thick. Place a tsp. of filling in center of each round. Bring three sides of the circle together in the middle to form a triangle. Pinch edges to seal. Let stand until doubled again. Brush tops with beaten egg. Place well spaced on greased baking sheets. Bake at 350 degrees until golden brown. (30-35 min)

This makes just over a dozen very large pastries. For smaller, make balls smaller.

Cookie Dough for Hamantaschen

4 eggs   1 lemon (juice and rind)
3/4 c. (150gr) melted shortening   4 c. sifted flour
3/4 c. (150gr) sugar   1/2 tsp. Sa
3 tsp. Baking powder

Combine first the eggs, shortening, lemon&flour. In large bowl beat until smooth. Sift together the dry ingredients and combine with the mixture until it forms balls of dough. Turn out onto board. Roll and cut into 2 1/2 in.
Rounds using a biscuit cutter. Place a rounded tablespoon of filling in the center and turn up the edges to form triangles making three seams. Start at top center and pinch together securely down toward the three corners. Brush tops with egg for glaze (optional) for 25-30 min. at 350 degrees until browned.

These freeze very well.

Fillings for Hamantaschen

Prune Filling

3 c. (750ml) finely chopped dried prunes
1/2 c. (125ml) nuts
juice and rind of one lemon
sugar to taste.

Combine all ingredients.

Poppy Seed (most traditional filling)
1 c. (250ml) poppy seed   pinch of salt
boiling water   1/2 c. (125ml) water
2 T. sugar   1/2 c. (125ml) finely chopped almonds
1/4 c. (60ml) honey

Pour boiling water over poppy seed and let stand until cool. Drain. Cook together poppy seed, sugar, honey, salt, and water over moderate heat until thick stirring frequently. Remove from heat and stir in chopped almonds. Cool.

"This is the way - walk ye in it.
Isaiah 30:21

Brachot

ברכות

PRAY
FOR THE PEACE
OF JERUSALEM

PS. 122:6

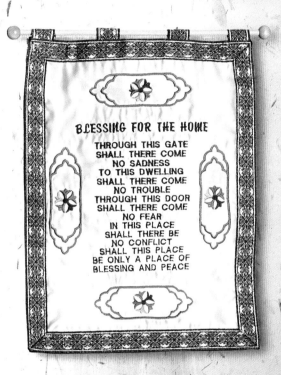

BLESSING FOR THE HOME

THROUGH THIS GATE
SHALL THERE COME
NO SADNESS
TO THIS DWELLING
SHALL THERE COME
NO TROUBLE
THROUGH THIS DOOR
SHALL THERE COME
NO FEAR
IN THIS PLACE
SHALL THERE BE
NO CONFLICT
SHALL THIS PLACE
BE ONLY A PLACE OF
BLESSING AND PEACE

The Lord
is my
shepherd;
I shall not want.

Psalms 23:1

As for me
and
my house,
we will serve
the Lord

Josh. 24:15

Blessings

Blessings are an integral part of Jewish daily life. From the moment of opening your eyes until going to sleep, there are blessings for virtually every act, deed, and sight. Blessings serve to remind us constantly of God's graciousness, mercy, and loving kindness.

It is our purpose here on earth to be able to raise the profane and mundane to holiness. Our spiritual compass keeps us on balance with God and his compassion.

"God has truly blessed me today". Recognizing God's participation in every facet of daily life surely effects not only our own selves but also impacts the lives of those with whom we come in contact.

Structure of a Blessing

What is the difference between a blessing and a prayer? In the daily prayer book with the order of morning, afternoon, and evening prayers, there are both prayers and blessings. A blessing will always be recognized by the introductory first six words:
Baruch ata, adonai eloheinu, melech ha'olam.
Blessed are you, O Lord our God, King of the Universe.
Following these six words will be the content of the blessing but the introduction is always the same.

Why?

These six words outline for us the multi-level relationship we acknowledge with God. Baruch ata....blessed are you.......This is my closest connection to the Almighty. I'm able to address you directly, Lord. This conversation is between the two of us....just you and me.
How marvelous to be able to acknowledge that the Holy One is so intimately accessible! Adonai eloheinu.....O Lord our God.... The word "our" is now plural. I have taken a step back to include myself as part of a people, all of whom recognize God as our communal strength. With this affirmation I acknowledge my responsibility not only to God but also to my fellow man.
Melech ha'olam.....King of the Universe. God is larger than just relating to me and my community. He is, indeed, ruler of the world!
I, also, am part of that world population. I recognize God's supremacy over any and all creation.
What an amazing concept! In six words, it is possible to thank, revere and recognize God even before giving a specific recognition in a specific blessing!

Here are some of the most commonly used daily blessings.

Shehechiyanu — Recited on the first time of doing anything...seeing a sunset for the day, eating a new fruit in its season, celebrating a family milestone, putting on a new dress, watching a child take its first step, etc. The list is endless!!!

ברוך אתה ה׳ אלוהינו מלך העולם שהחיינו וקיימנו והגיענו לזמן הזה.

Baruch ata adonai, eloheinu melech ha'olam, shehechiyanu, v'kiyamanu, v'higiyanu l'zman hazeh.

Blessed are you, O Lord our God, King of the Universe who has kept us in life, and sustained us , and allowed us to reach this moment.

Motzi - Recited before eating bread

ברוך אתה ה׳ אלוהינו מלך העולם המוציא לחם מן הארץ.

Baruch ata adonai, eloheinu melech ha'olam, hamotzi lechem min ha'aretz.

Blessed are you, O Lord our God, King of the Universe, who brings forth bread from the earth.

Netilat Yadaim.....Washing the hands

ברוך אתה ה׳ אלוהינו מלך העולם אשר קדשנו במצוותיו וצוונו על נטילת ידיים.

Baruch ata adonai, eloheinu melech ha'olam, asher kidshanu b'mitzvotav, v'tzivanu al netilat yadayim.

Blessed are you, O Lord our God, King of the Universe who has sanctified us with commandments and commanded us about washing the hands.

Kol B'dvaro....When eating a meal (or snack) that does not include bread.

ברוך אתה ה׳ אלוהינו מלך העולם שהכל נהיה בדברו.

Baruch ata adonai, eloheinu melech ha'olam sh'hakol n'heeyeh b'dvaro.

Blessed are you, O Lord our God, King of the Universe through whose word all things came into being.

M'zonot....When eating food other than bread made from any of the other grains...barley, rye, oats, wheat, spelt, rice.

ברוך אתה ה׳ אלוהינו מלך העולם בורא מיני מזונות.

Baruch ata adonai, eloheinu melech ha'olam boray menay m'zonot.

Blessed are you, O Lord our God, King of the Universe who creates all types of food.

Ha'adamah.....Eating   a vegetable or fruit coming from the ground

ברוך אתה ה׳ אלוהינו מלך העולם בורא פרי האדמה.

Baruch ata adonai, eloheinu melech ha'olam, boray pree ha'adamah

Blessed are you, O Lord our God, King of the Universe who brings forth food from the ground.

Pree ha'etz....Eating a fruit from the tree

ברוך אתה ה׳ אלוהינו מלך העולם בורא פרי העץ.

Baruch ata adonai, eloheinu melech ha'olam boray pree ha'etz.

Blessed are you, O Lord our God, King of the Universe, who creates the fruit of the tree.

There are blessings that cover every aspect of our lives but these are a good start!!

There is no reason why we can't use any or all of these blessings whenever the occasion warrants. Taking time to thank God for all the little things we daily encounter will constantly remind us before whom we stand.

The First Morning Prayer - Modeh Ani

מודה אני לפניך מלך חי וקים, שהחזרת בי נשמתי בחמלה רבה אמונתך.

Modeh ani lifanecha, melech chai vkayam, shehechezarta bee nishmati, bchemlah rabah emunatecha.

I confess before you and thank you, O Living King, that in great mercy and faithfulness you have returned unto me my soul.

This prayer, recited even before getting out of bed, thanks God for His faithfulness to us, keeping our souls safe during the long night and returning it to us from His watch in great mercy. How beautiful it is, that despite our misdeeds or thoughts of the day before, the Almighty has given us a fresh day, a new start, a clean slate whereon we can write our daily activities dedicated to Him.

Tefillin

תפילין

Tefillin

Upon reaching adulthood, at age 13, boys put on the phylacteries (Greek) known in Hebrew as Tefillin.

It is based on a Biblical commandment from Deuteronomy 6:4-9, the prayer known as the Shema.

The Shema is the watchword of the Jewish people saying: Hear, O Israel, the Lord our God, the Lord is one. (Deut. 6:4)

It goes on to say: You shall bind them for a sign upon your hand and they shall be for frontlets between your eyes.

This passage testifies to the eternal covenant between God and Israel. With the tefillin, the Jewish male identifies with his Jewish past, present, and future.

This is, by the way, the same passage that is placed inside the mezuzah on the doorpost.

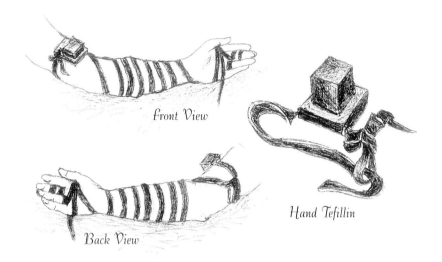

Front View

Back View

Hand Tefillin

What do they look like?

Each of the two tefillin is a square box with long straps attached. One is placed on the head, the other on the arm.

In the box that is attached to the head, there are four separate compartments. Each has a Hebrew quotation placed within the compartment. The first bids us to remember their freedom from slavery and to celebrate the Passover. (Exodus 13:1-10) The second refers to the redemption of the first-born. (Exodus 13:11-16) The third and fourth compartments contain two sections of the Shema prayer from Deuteronomy (6:4-9 and 11:13-20)

The armpiece has only one strap with all four sections written on it.

Each box has been imprinted with the Hebrew letters, Shin, Daled, and Yod, which spells Shaddai, an acronym for God's most mystical name.

Tefillin are worn only on weekdays and not on Shabbat or Festivals, because the latter are in themselves reminders of the covenant between God and Israel.

The tefillin for the arm are on the left arm, close to the heart. It is wrapped seven times around the forearm below the elbow. The remaining strap is put around the palm of the hand.

The tefillin for the head are placed on the forehead between the eyes. The knot of the head strap is at the base of the skull, and the straps are then brought forward across the chest, lying loosely.

Now, the strap around the palm of the hand is unwrapped and wound three times around the middle finger. The remainder is carried around the ring finger and then rewound around the palm.

As with the tallit, there would be no requirement for you to wear the tefillin. However, for general knowledge or demonstration, it could be useful.

You may want to own and wear them during your own personal prayer time.

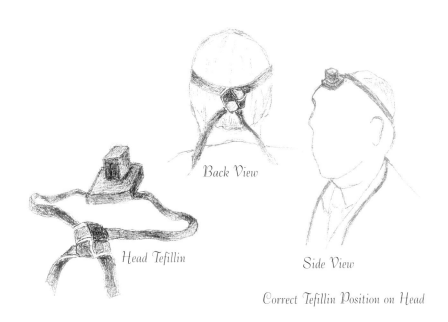

Head Tefillin

Back View

Side View

Correct Tefillin Position on Head

The Seven Species

שבעת המינים

The Seven Species

When the Lord brings the children of Israel into the land, he tells them:

"For the Lord your God is bringing you into a good land, a land of brooks of water, of fountains and springs, that flow out of valley and hills; a land of WHEAT and BARLEY, of VINES and FIG trees and POMEGRANATES, a land of OLIVE OIL and HONEY"

Each of the above mentioned items are indigenous to the Land of Israel and have provided over the millennia the lushness and richness in the land.

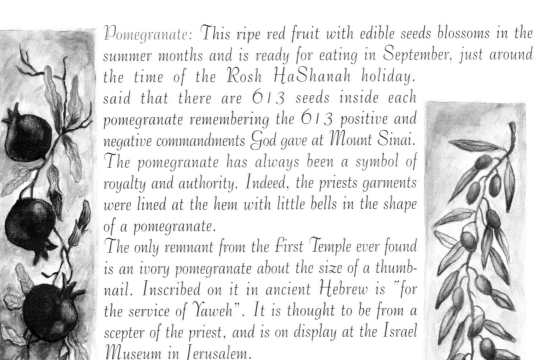

Pomegranate: This ripe red fruit with edible seeds blossoms in the summer months and is ready for eating in September, just around the time of the Rosh HaShanah holiday. said that there are 613 seeds inside each pomegranate remembering the 613 positive and negative commandments God gave at Mount Sinai. The pomegranate has always been a symbol of royalty and authority. Indeed, the priests garments were lined at the hem with little bells in the shape of a pomegranate.

The only remnant from the First Temple ever found is an ivory pomegranate about the size of a thumbnail. Inscribed on it in ancient Hebrew is "for the service of Yaweh". It is thought to be from a scepter of the priest, and is on display at the Israel Museum in Jerusalem.

Biblical references to the pomegranate: Ex. 28:33
I Kings 7:20

Olive oil: The olive tree can live for hundreds and hundreds of years and continually bear fruit. As one of the main crops of the land of Israel, it was carefully nurtured to provide both the fruit and the oil to the ancient world.

Since the major value of the olive is the oil, and thirty percent of the oil is in the pit, both the pulp and pit must be crushed and pressed to achieve maximum value. There are four main pressings for the olive.

The first pressing: this is the cleanest and purest oil. It was used for anointing of kings and priests. The first pressing is also known as virgin olive oil.

The second pressing: this, also, is exceptionally fine and clean. It is used for cooking and eating.

The third pressing: By the third pressing, little bits of pit and pulp filter into the oil but it is still good for making soap and cleaning objects.

The fourth pressing: At the last pressing the oil is already "dirty" but still usable. It was used for light in oil lamps. That's why if you purchase an ancient oil lamp, you will generally find some soot around the wick area from the burning of dirty oil.

Biblical references: I Samuel 10:1, I Kings 6:23

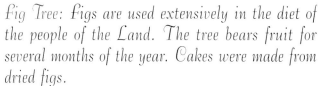

Fig Tree: Figs are used extensively in the diet of the people of the Land. The tree bears fruit for several months of the year. Cakes were made from dried figs.

The Biblical idea of peace and prosperity was portrayed as:

"....everyone able to sit down under their own vine and fig tree."

Biblical reference: Amos 7:14, Luke 19:4

Date Palm: The date palm grows exceedingly tall and straight with the fruit blossoming under huge leaves, hanging in long clusters. Today some breeds of date palms are able to produce between two hundred and two hundred fifty kilos of dates per tree per year!! When Jesus rode into Jerusalem, the people greeted him waving date palm leaves.

Biblical reference: John 12:13

The Vine: Referring to grape vines, this is one of the most important fruit crops in the Land. Depending on the part of the country wherein the vines were planted, some were low to the ground on rocky terrain and some were grown on trailers above the ground. At harvest time, grapes were crushed in the wine presses by barefoot workers, crushing the pulp but not the seed of the grape which would make the wine bitter. Some juices were used immediately as a drink while some were put into skins and left to ferment and mature into fine wine. Today, some of Israel's finest wines are grown on the Golan Heights where warm days and cool or cold nights are perfect for producing sweet wines.

Biblical reference: Jesus described the grape vine in 5 parables and called himself the true vine on which the branches depend. Matthew 9: 17

Wheat and Barley: The basic grains used for daily diet in ancient times. The mainstay of the diet of the people of Galilee in Jesus' day was barley bread and salted fish. Jesus tells his disciples, "I am the bread of life."

Biblical reference: Multiplication of loaves and fishes: Matthew 14: 15-21.

The Breastplate

The priests wore special garments which were woven in a proscribed manner from five materials: gold threads, techelet (a particular shade of blue)wool, dark red wool, crimson wool and twisted linen.

The High Priest wore both an ephod and breastplate made of all five materials. "And they shall make the ephod of gold, of blue, and of purple, of scarlet, and fine twined linen, with cunning work" (Ex. 28:26)

"And thou shalt make the breastplate of judgment with cunning work; after the work

of the ephod thou shalt make it; of gold, of blue, and of purple, and of scarlet, and of fine twined linen, shalt thou make it" (Ex 28:15

The ephod and the breastplate were always worn together: indeed, attached to each other so a word about the ephod is in order.

The ephod was worn covering the back of the body as a type of skirt from just below the elbows to the heel. It was tied in front with a belt and had straps coming up the back and over the shoulders.
At the shoulder were placed onyx stones on which were engraved the names of the tribes of Israel. These two onyx stones were called "remembrance stones". The High Priest carries the tribes names before God, and the children of Israel, seeing their names inscribed would be reminded of God's instructions to them.

Directly under the onyx stones, two square gold settings were affixed to the shoulders. The rings of the breastplate were attached to these gold settings by gold chains.

As for the breastplate itself: it was set with four rows of precious stones, three stones in each row. On each stone was engraved the name of the twelve sons of Jacob. The exact identification of each stone has eluded scholars to this day. The Hebrew names of these stones are not commonly used and no description of them appears elsewhere in Scripture.

Nonetheless, the stones are identified as follows:
Row one: colored crystal, topaz, ruby
Row two: emerald, sapphire, diamond

Row three: ligure, agate, amethyst
Row four: beryl, onyx, jasper.
The colors of the twelve stones also became the colors of the identifying banners of each tribe. Down through the ages royal families and families of great prominence developed family crests on banners by which they could be identified. It's Biblical! Numbers 22 tells us: "Every man shall be by his banner, according to his paternal family."

As for the tribes, it is as follows:
Reuben, the ruby, has a red banner with an emblem showing the mandrakes he would bring to his mother. (Gen.30:14)
Shimon, the emerald,has a green banner with a picture of Shechem in remembrance of what he'd done there. (Gen. 24:25).
Levi, a tri-colored crystal, has a banner of red, white, and black. On the banner was the breastplate of the priests, since the priests come from the tribe of Levi.
Judah, the carbuncle, has a banner of light blue with a picture of a lion. (Gen. 49:9)
Issachar, a sapphire, has a banner of dark blue with a picture of the sun and moon. Astronomers of reknown were in the tribe of Issachar. (I Chronicles 12:33)
Zebulun, on a diamond , has a banner of white with a picture of a ship. This tribe was dedicated to fishing and sailing and sea commerce. (Gen.49:13)
Dan, a topaz, has a dark blue banner with a picture of a snake, from "Let Dan be a serpent on the path." (Gen. 49:17)
Gad, an agate, has a black and white banner with a picture of an army tent. (Gen.49:19)
Naphtali, ligure, a light red stone, with a figure of the gazelle. Naphtali was said to be swift of foot. (Gen.49:21)
Asher, a blackish yellow stone, has a banner with an emblem of an olive tree. (Gen. 49:20)
Joseph, an onyx, has a banner of jet black with an emblem showing the two half tribes of Mannaseh and Ephraim.
Benjamin, a jasper, has a multicouloured banner with the emblem of a wolf cub, for he was the baby of the family and cared for by all his brothers. (Gen. 49:27

There was also a mystical aspect to the breastplate. "And thou shalt put in the breastplate of judgment the Urim and the Tummim; and they shall be upon Aaron's heart, when he goeth in before the Lord". (Ex. 28:30)
Most biblical scholars hold that the Urim and the Tummim were NOT the breastplate

itself but rather the divine mystical name of God. This name was written on a piece of parchment and inserted into the flap of the garment. It was an oracle-like aspect of the breastplate by which the High Priest could receive answers to important questions.

Applications for you.

We don't have today a breastplate but artisans today have created very beautiful jewelry...rings and pendants in the form of the breastplate. It's a lovely gift with Biblical interest attached to it!

The Jewish Calendar

לוח שנה עברי

"Ask for the peace of Jerusalem"

"שאלו שלום ירושלים" תהלים קכ״ב

The Jewish Calendar

The Jewish calendar as we know it today is a unique combination of the solar year and lunar months.

The earliest Hebrew calendar known to us was found in the excavations at the ancient city of Gezer (near the modern city of Tel Aviv). It was written on a clay tablet in ancient Hebrew script. The part that could be deciphered was as follows:

"A month of fruit harvest. A month of sowing. A month of after-grass. A month of flax harvest. A month of barley harvest. A month of everything else. A month of vine pruning. A month of fig harvest."

This seems to have come into being after people became settled and worked in agriculture. Until then, nomads traveling seemed to be more cognizant of seasons rather than months. Winter meant rain. Summer meant lack of rain. Years were counted by the sun. People realized there were times when the days were longer and times when they were shorter.

Graduallly, the period of time it takes for the moon to travel around the earth became known as a month. The Hebrew word for month is Hodesh whose root means "new". A month became the period of time between new moons.

A lunar month is 29 days, 12 hours, and 44 minutes. A lunar year is twelve months containing 354 days, 8 hours and 48 minutes. This makes it about 11 days shorter than the solar year of 365 days, 12 hours and 49 minutes. An adjustment must be made so that the holidays follow at the affixed time given us by God.

Deuteronomy 16:1 " You shall observe the month of springtime and perform the pesach-offering for the Lord, your God, for in the month of springtime the Lord, your God, took you out of Egypt at night."

Numbers 9:1-3 " The Lord spoke to Moses, in the Wilderness of Sinai, in the second year from heir exodus from the land of Egypt, in the first month, saying: "The Children of Israel shall make the Pesach-offering in tis appointed time. On the fourteenth day of this month in the afternoon shall you make it, in its appointed time; according to all its decrees and laws shall you make it."

To make sure the holidays fall at the appointed time, a plan for leap years was established. It was determined that in a cycle of 19 years, 7 leap years would occur with an additional month added, called Adar Sheni, Second Adar. These would fall on the 3rd, 6th, 8th, 11th, 14th, 17th, and 19th year of each cycle.

Five months have 30 days, five months have 29 days and two months vary from year to year.

The names of the Hebrew months with their holidays are as follows:
Nissan - Passover
Iyar - Memorial Day, Israel Independence Day, Lag B'Omer
Sivan - Shavuot
Tammuz
Av - Tisha B'Av (Destruction of both the First and Second Temples)
Elul
Tishri - Rosh HaShanah, Yom Kippur, Sukkot
Heshvan
Kislev - Chanukah
Tevet

Shevat - Tu b'shevat (Birthday of the trees)
Adar - Purim. In Leap years, Purim is celebrated in Second Adar.

There are no names to the days of the week. We follow the creation story as God calls the days, Day one, Day two, etc. Only the seventh day has a name Shabbat. It was on this day that God rested from all his work and creation.

The Jewish calendar we use today was codified by Hillel the Second about 1600 years ago. It is today the most accurate for gauging the passage of time. Indeed, in Maimonides' calculations to the millionth of seconds, the hour divided into 1080 parts turns out to be the final calculations achieved by NASA scientists when determining precise timing for space travel. It was all clarified so long ago!

"Therefore thou shalt keep the commandments of the Lord thy God, to walk in his ways and to fear him."

Deuteronomy 8:6

About the author

Born and raised in Boston, educated at University of Hartford, Boston Hebrew College, and Hebrew University, Susan taught Russian Jewish History, Holocaust , and Hebrew studies in the Jewish school system of greater Hartford, Connecticut. After making aliyah, (immigrating to Israel) in 1977, she became a licensed tour guide. Specializing in Biblical and archaeological studies, the State of Israel has often featured her to represent them on teaching tours. She has been interviewed regularly by television and radio as well as many newspapers concerning the current events in the Middle East.

Susan and her husband Aaron live in the Biblical city of Modi'in where she actively continues her ministry of teaching throughout the land of Israel.

Susan Marcus
E-mail: srmcom@netvision.net il